Original title:
Twigs and Terse Verses

Copyright © 2025 Creative Arts Management OÜ
All rights reserved.

Author: Vivienne Beaumont
ISBN HARDBACK: 978-1-80567-172-5
ISBN PAPERBACK: 978-1-80567-471-9

Silent Stanzas Among the Shrubs

A leaf once tried to tell a joke,
But tangled in the limbs, it choked.
The laughter rustled in the breeze,
And squirrels snickered from the trees.

The bushes giggled, tickled pink,
As blossoms wobbled on the brink.
Each berry burst with silent glee,
In this shy grove, so wild and free.

Concise Notes in the Bark

A message carved, 'Hello, I'm here,'
By a beetle full of cheer.
He scribbled fast, his legs so quick,
But misspelled 'wood' as 'woody slick.'

The trees all chuckled, branches swayed,
As creatures danced in sun's parade.
With every knot, a story told,
In laughter lines, the bark turned bold.

Hushed Whispers of the Understory

Fungi gossiped in the gloom,
They'd share a tale, then swiftly zoom.
A snail with dreams of being fast,
Claimed he could win a race at last.

But in the shade, the mushrooms grinned,
'Let's see that speed, your chance rescind!'
As shadows shared a wink and nod,
The forest floor played silent god.

Imprints on the Forest Floor

A critter danced with tiny paws,
Leaving prints like tangled straws.
But every step was such a blunder,
As he tripped on roots and rolled like thunder.

The ferns just shook their leafy heads,
While laughing at the path he treads.
In nature's play, a merry spree,
The forest laughed in harmony.

Conserved Words Among the Flora

In the garden of chatter, they prune with care,
Each syllable clipped, like a wild-haired hare.
Petals gossip quietly, in giggling grace,
While bees buzz by, wearing a sunny face.

Leaves exchange secrets in the soft breeze,
Whispers of wisdom, if you please.
A daisy's bad joke makes the roses blush,
Even cacti roll laughter, in a silent hush.

The Geometry of Leaves and Lines

Measure the puns in each shaped leaf,
Angles of humor defy all belief.
A triangle giggles with a quadrants' jest,
While circles swirl softly, trying their best.

Each line softly curves, like a winding trail,
Telling tall tales with a laughable fail.
Math-mirth grows louder as seasons unwind,
Numbers and nature in sync, intertwined.

Wooded Reflections in Echoed Simplicity

In the woods, a mirror reflects some wit,
Where trees chuckle gently, their branches split.
A birch cracks a joke at the oak's expense,
While pine needles snicker, all in good sense.

Reeds whisper riddles that dance on the air,
Echoed simplicity, a giggle to share.
Beneath the broad canopy, hidden delight,
Foliage frolics in the dappled light.

The Minimalist's Garden of Rhymes

Less is more, shouts the dainty sprout,
Words distilled down, like a wise old scout.
In this simple plot, where humor's concise,
Each chuckle is planted, precise and nice.

A lone petunia dispenses its cheer,
While daisies stand tall, making lines clear.
Gardening laughter in rows that are neat,
Where rhymes bloom brightly, short and sweet.

Dancing Shadows and Crisp Consonants

In a world where shadows play,
They wiggle and jive, come what may.
With letters that hop to their own beat,
They twist and turn on tiny feet.

A consonant dance, so sharp and bright,
Whispering jokes in the pale moonlight.
Syllables giggle in a whimsical way,
As laughter echoes at the end of the day.

The Essence of Earth in Evocative Phrases

Under the ground, where secrets sleep,
Earth chuckles softly, hidden and deep.
Phrases pop up like daisies at noon,
Holding their breath as they burst into tune.

With every word, the soil turns gold,
Funny little stories just waiting to be told.
Roots tickle each other, a mischievous play,
As nature giggles the whole live-long day.

Branches of Breezy Whispers

Branches bend low, with secrets to share,
Rustling their leaves, without a care.
Whispers float high, like candy on air,
Sneaking up close, to catch you unaware.

A breeze full of chuckles, tickling your cheek,
Branches break out in laughter, so unique.
They tell of the sun and all it unfurls,
In giggles and sighs, in spirals and twirls.

The Quiet Sketches of Nature

In the quiet of green where humor hides,
Nature doodles with whimsical strides.
Each petal, a pun, each stem, a delight,
Drawing smiles softly, both day and night.

The whispers of forests sketch tales anew,
With every rustle, a giggle or two.
Even the rocks have stories to weave,
In the quiet of nature, it's hard to believe!

The Humble Hymns of the Harvest

In fields so wide, the veggies dance,
Carrots waltz, with no second chance.
Tomatoes giggle, in a ripe parade,
Chased by the beet, with a jester's charade.

Pumpkins plot with a smile so bright,
Squash joins in, a delightful sight.
Corn's fluffy hair, a wig of delight,
Brought laughter as they swayed through the night.

The sun is cracking, rays start to beam,
Potatoes sing loud, as they form a team.
With every pluck, a joke is delivered,
Nature's harvest, hilariously quivered.

When the day ends, in the twilight glow,
Vegetables bow, it's time for the show.
With laughter echoing, through the cool air,
Fruits and greens, a merry affair.

Charted Silence Among the Thorns

In the thicket where the roses tease,
Thorns sit grumpy, never say please.
Branches argue, who's the fanciest flower,
Petals snicker, in their fragrant power.

Budding thoughts buzz, like bees in a hive,
Juicy jests keep the garden alive.
Tulips chuckle, bending low in glee,
Daffodils dance, but with zero decree.

Among the fuss, the weeds look askew,
Sharing stories that are far from true.
A sunflower snorts, with seeds in its head,
While ladybugs giggle, and roll over bed.

As dusk settles in, shadows grow long,
Nature's party, where all belong.
In the silent thorns, the laughter ignites,
Even the cacti find joy in the nights.

The Succinct Story of Sprouts

In a garden patch, tiny seeds appear,
Sprouts crack jokes, full of good cheer.
Whispers of growth, all around spread,
A radish claims it's the king of the bed.

The peas are giggling, just hanging out,
Watching the lettuce, in laughter, they shout.
With vibrant greens, they play peek-a-boo,
Every tiny sprout, a comedian too.

Tiny roots tickle, down in the dirt,
As radishes boast in their bubblegum shirt.
Playing tag with the worms, oh what a race,
Nature's comedy fills up the space.

When the sun sets, and stars peek bright,
Sprouts share secrets in the soft moonlight.
A comedy club, beneath the green skies,
Where laughter blooms and grows, oh how it flies!

Remnants of Rhythm in the Woods

In the thick of the woods, the creatures collide,
Squirrels play drums, with acorns as pride.
Bears hum tunes, with their grizzly flair,
Owls provide wisdom, but seldom care.

With branches that sway, a soft song unfolds,
Foxes share fables, as the night grows cold.
Moonbeams join in, with a wink and a glow,
Every bark and chirp, like a stand-up show.

In the hush of the night, shadows fool around,
Mischief is brewing, in sounds that abound.
Crickets tap dance, as fireflies twirl,
Creating a ballet, in this woodland whirl.

As dawn breaks anew, the symphony fades,
Each critter retreats, from their playful charades.
Yet whispers linger, through the morning's wood,
In the heart of the forest, laughter once stood.

The Sparse Chorus of Chickadees

In the trees, they chirp and sway,
Chickadees dance, making their play.
Who knew small birds could joke so loud?
A fleeting audience, a feathered crowd.

With a hop and a flutter, they strut their stuff,
If only life were this easy, and never tough.
Beaks are open, riffs they share,
In the thicket, laughter fills the air.

They sing of crumbs and sunlit snacks,
Counting their cheer in little quacks.
A light-hearted chorus, swift and spry,
In nature's stage, they aim and fly.

So heed the call, if you can catch,
The feathered fables, they'll never match.
For in their tunes, joy takes flight,
In the leafy audience, it's pure delight.

Nature's Quiet Composition

Amidst the green, a symphony plays,
Leaves rustle softly, in nature's ways.
A twig snaps here, a whisper there,
Each moment's laughter floats in the air.

Clouds drift by, with a giggle or two,
Sunbeam chuckles, as if it knew.
Breezes tickle, trees sway along,
Creating a melody, light and strong.

Little critters add their own tunes,
Frogs croak proudly beneath the moons.
The nightingale hums, a playful shout,
In nature's fun, there's never a doubt.

So close your eyes, let the laughter seep,
Feel the rhythm that cradles sleep.
Nature composes, both silly and wise,
In this green hall, laughter never dies.

Splinters of Sound in the Stillness

A crack here and there, not quite serene,
Snap of a branch, sly and keen.
In silence, laughter often grows,
As the playful wind brings comic prose.

Rustling grass, a giggly tease,
Innocent whispers carried with ease.
Nature's humor, so bold and true,
As squirrels prank with a raucous crew.

A stream gurgles secrets, oh so sly,
While high-flying birds just zoom by.
Laughter stitched in every sound,
In the heart of the woods, joy is found.

So listen closely, oh curious friend,
There's laughter in nature, around every bend.
In splinters of sound, a joy revealed,
In the stillness of life, hilarity is healed.

Brevity Beneath Boughs

Underneath branches, short and stout,
Whispers of humor flit about.
Tiny jokes from critters so small,
Laughter echoes, a thriving call.

A squirrel stumbles, all in a dash,
Chasing its tail, in a bumbling flash.
The trees chuckle, they sway and grin,
At the sight of mischief, where chaos begins.

The sun peeks through in playful spots,
Trickling down on all the knots.
In this brevity, joy finds a way,
Under the boughs, where we all play.

So take a moment, pause for a laugh,
Life's silly antics are here on the path.
For within the shade, we'll always find,
The joy of laughter, so cleverly twined.

Delicate Verses on Twisted Limbs

A branch bent down to joke,
A squirrel chuckled loud.
It dropped its acorn shell,
Landed right on my crown.

The leaves all giggled too,
Swishing in the breeze.
Nature's jester crew,
Cracking up with ease.

Each twist a punchline framed,
In whispers from the trees.
I'm the one who's blamed,
As bark hides laughter's tease.

So here I take the bow,
To jesters of the wood.
Thank you for the show,
You wild, leafy brood.

Shards of Light Through Canopy

Sunbeams poke and prod,
Like kids at play,
They dance on mossy clods,
Chasing shadows away.

A squirrel smirks in shade,
With acorns in his hands.
He thinks he's got it made,
In his leafy, nutty lands.

Laughter echoes high,
From branches lanky tall.
Nature can't deny,
It's a humorous brawl.

Through gaps the sun spills gold,
Making serfs of the green.
Every story told,
From where I'm seen, a queen.

The Unspoken Lore of Ferns

In the shadow's curl,
Ferns gossip quite a lot.
Whispers whirl and swirl,
In their polka-dot plot.

A dandelion chimes in,
With a puff of wit.
It spins a tale of kin,
While ferns just laugh and sit.

As fronds sway to and fro,
They trade their secret dreams.
Their roots connect below,
Like giggles in moonbeams.

So when you wander past,
Listen for the fun.
In the quiet cast,
Laughter's never done.

Wists of Wind in the Thicket

A breeze danced through the leaves,
   Tickling branches so free.
   With rustles, it achieves,
   A joke from tree to tree.

   Behind a bush, a shout,
   A rabbit's chuckle flies.
   It peeks and hops about,
     A playful surprise.

   The thicket whispers low,
  With tales of wind and whim.
  Where laughter seems to grow,
    In shadows, it won't dim.

   Oh, if you tread with care,
  You'll hear the nature's glee.
   From secret spots, beware,
  You might just join the spree!

Whispers from Splintered Branches

A stick once had a chat,
With a leaf that flew too low,
"You're funny, oh so spry!"
"I'm grounded; you can go!"

They giggled in the breeze,
As shadows danced all around,
Each branch a witness here,
To leavings without a sound.

The ants began to waltz,
In twirls around the roots,
"Is that a twig I see?"
"Oh no, it's just the new shoots!"

Nature loves a sweet joke,
With whispers through the glade,
Laughter echoes from bark,
In silence, merriment played.

Fractured Lines in Nature's Tongue

A twig cracked up while leaning,
With laughter, quite the scene,
"Can you believe the fall?"
"Next time, wear some green!"

The rocks just shook their heads,
While the grass just rolled its eyes,
When vines began to truss,
And laughter filled the skies.

Every shrub joined the jest,
In jest, they waved around,
Poking fun at the roots,
Growing low to the ground.

Amongst the sunlit leaves,
Where giggles twist and sway,
Each nature's tiny spark,
Keeps boredom far away.

The Echo of Shortened Stems

In silence, stems conspire,
To share a comical tale,
"Watch me stretch to the sun!"
"Only if you don't fail!"

They swayed under the weight,
Of stories great and bold,
While petals burst with laughter,
As they shared the old, old gold.

A whisper from a bud,
"Look at me, all new and bright!"
"They said I'm just a sprout,"
"Just a smaller version, right?"

In every crack and crevice,
Humor blooms and gleams,
In nature's loudest whispers,
Reality's just dreams.

Minimalist Musings Beneath the Bark

Underneath the rough crust,
Lies a world both strange and neat,
Where bugs tell silly riddles,
While the roots dance on their feet.

A snail slid up to cheer,
"I move at lightning speed!"
The woodpecker chuckled loud,
"Snails, that sounds like a creed!"

Tiny sprites among the leaves,
Wove tales of leaves and rain,
Each drop a wink to us,
A secret held, yet plain.

So gather round the bark,
Where humor's subtly found,
In nature's quirky scrapes,
Joy and laughter abound.

The Whispering Archive of the Trees

In the breeze, secrets flow,
Leaves gossip soft and low.
Branches sway with tales in flight,
Bark chuckles in the moonlight.

A squirrel snickers, gathering nuts,
While the owl hoots, 'What the guts?'
Raccoons play cards with fallen seeds,
Nature's jest in leafy deeds.

Roots tickle soil, giggling deep,
While shadows dance, never sleep.
Frisky winds tease the rustling boughs,
As trees chuckle their ancient vows.

Oh, what a ruckus in the shade,
Where echoes of laughter never fade.
Laughter lingers on every ring,
In the archive where the treefolk sing.

Snippets of Serenity Underneath the Sky

Clouds drift like dreams on a spree,
Birds chirp jokes, oh so carefree.
Grass sways, joining in the jest,
Nature giggles, it knows best.

A flower sticks out its tiny tongue,
While the sun rays dance, a song unsung.
Bees buzz about with a playful sting,
Collecting laughter, the sweetest thing.

Breezy whispers tickle the leaves,
As butterflies weave funny reprieves.
Echos of glee in every petal,
Creating joy on a sunny meddle.

Underneath this wide, bright dome,
Every creature feels right at home.
So let us laugh until we sigh,
In snippets of peace beneath the sky.

The Parable of the Petiole

A petiole said to a proud leaf,
'Without me, you'd face some grief!'
'Think of the times I hold you tight,
Makin' sure you catch the light.'

But the leaf replied with a grin,
'Thank you, friend, for the support win.'
'Together we sway, what a happy pair,
Dancing in breezes without a care.'

Then came a gust, fierce and strong,
Twisting and turning, all went wrong!
Yet, they giggled and clung with glee,
For this tussle was a sight to see.

A lesson learned, both would agree,
In the dance of life, just let it be.
To pals who share the laugh and play,
Every petiole's worth the fray.

Palimpsest in the Pine

Oh pine tree tall, with layers deep,
You hide old stories, secrets keep.
Each ring a chapter, every scar,
A legacy beneath the stars.

Squirrels etch their paths like prose,
While down below, a snail's tale grows.
Nature's canvas, a funny script,
In each knot, a giggle's quipped.

Wind whispers jokes to branches high,
While needles brush against the sky.
The pine chuckles, a wise old sage,
In the book of life, it turns the page.

With every breeze, a laugh unfurls,
In the forest's heart, joy twirls.
For in each twist and twine of vine,
Life writes its whims, in every pine.

Echoes of Leaves in Twilight

In the hush of twilight's grace,
The leaves laugh, keep up the pace.
Crickets chirp a silly tune,
While owls debate 'Who's the buffoon?'

Squirrels play a hide-and-seek,
Their acorns roll, oh what a peek!
With shadows dancing on the ground,
The giggles of dusk knows no bound.

Thistle and Tinctures of Time

A thistle pricks a passing thought,
While time giggles, oh what a plot!
The clock winks, does a little jest,
As flowers bloom in polka-dots dressed.

Caterpillars make a silly fuss,
Wiggling slow on a crowded bus.
They refuse to take a straight line,
In the waltz of a whimsical design.

Rippled Reflections of Resilience

Ponds chuckle as they shimmer bright,
Reflecting clouds in a playful fight.
Fish leap high, then splash with glee,
Yelling, 'Catch that ripple, it's free!'

The lily pads wear crowns each day,
While frogs croak songs in their ballet.
With each splash, a chuckle we hear,
Nature's jokes keep us all near.

Minimal Melodies in the Marsh

In the marsh, a melody sings,
With bullfrogs dressed in tiny rings.
A dragonfly spins a web of cheer,
   Dodging reeds without a fear.

The mudfish flaunts a tail like art,
While water lilies play their part.
Each ripple creates a comic scene,
Where laughter flows, it's evergreen.

Lyrical Labyrinths of Leaflets

In a garden full of green,
A lettuce tried to dance and preen.
With every slip and foolish spin,
It laughed at all the bees' chagrin.

The tomatoes watched with eyes so wide,
As cucumbers took a goofy slide.
An onion joined, but cried a tear,
Its layers peeled with every cheer.

A radish burst with vibrant glee,
Claiming it was king, just wait and see.
The carrots chuckled, knowing the truth,
In this green hijinks, we find the youth.

So here's to veggies, funny and bright,
In their little world, what a hilarious sight!

The Subtle Symphony of Stone and Soil

In the park where pebbles mutter,
A stone once claimed it knew the utter.
It spoke in rhymes, quite proud and bold,
Yet tripped on roots it couldn't hold.

The soil sighed, with patience stout,
As daisies teased the stones about.
"Are you tough?" they dared to say,
"Or just a rock that's stuck in clay?"

A nearby snail began to hum,
With every note, the stones went numb.
But then the ants formed a parade,
"Join us, stones!" they sang, unafraid!

Now every rock just shakes its head,
Joining the tune, no longer dread.
In laughter's echo, they find their flair,
In a symphony of soil and stone, they share!

Quickened Quips of the Quagmire

In a bog where frogs regale,
A puddle sprouted, looking pale.
It tried to host a fancy ball,
But water lilies took the fall.

The ducks quacked jokes that flew too high,
While mudbugs plotted wry and sly.
"What's a puddle's favorite game?"
"Squish and splash!" they cheered in fame!

A nearby turtle grinned with pride,
Wearing a mossy crown, he'd glide.
"Let's dance!" he said, then slipped a bit,
A flip, a flop, but never quit!

With every tumble, the laughter rang,
In the quagmire, joy brightly sang.
So let's embrace the messy fun,
Where every slip brings room to run!

Slices of Sound Among the Cedars

In a forest filled with cedar trees,
The branches whispered jokes with ease.
A squirrel piped in, "I've got a pun!"
"Why did the acorn never run?"

"Because it didn't want to be a nut!"
Laughed a bird who flew a little strut.
A breeze danced through, spinning tales,
Of pinecone pirates and their sails.

Deer with a wink joined the banter,
"Watch out for those saplings, they can ganter!"
A mouse squeaked back, "I'll get my cheese,
To have a feast beneath the trees!"

So in the woods, where echoes blend,
Each creature's laughter has no end.
In this orchestra of winks and giggles,
Life's a series of joyful wiggles!

Echoes of the Forest's Quiet Words

In whispers soft, the trees do talk,
A squirrel pauses, checking his clock.
With acorns scattered, plans they devise,
While pondering life with playful sighs.

A crow caws loudly, a mockery cheer,
As leaves giggle low, secrets to share.
Fungi jest with their cap and their stem,
Staging a play, we're all part of them.

The brook chuckles, bubbling along,
As critters join in with a harmonious song.
Each branch a joke, every root a pun,
Nature's humor, oh, such silly fun!

So gather 'round, dear friend and mate,
In the forest's riddle, join in the fate.
With laughter and joy, let spirits lift,
In the woods of whimsy, consider this gift.

Minimalism Amidst the Woodlands

Just one twig, but oh what a line,
Noble in stance, standing so fine.
A leaf flutters down, wears a grin,
Crafting a story, where should we begin?

Branches wave, they say 'Hello',
With minimal words, their secrets flow.
Mushrooms peek, they share a glance,
In the quiet space, nature's romance.

A bobcat stretches, filling the void,
With gestures grand, yet so little cloyed.
No need for much, just playful winks,
In the wild where the humor links.

In this place of whispers and cheer,
The simple truths become quite clear.
Brevity reigns, brief tales arise,
In minimalism, laughter's the prize.

Threads of Thought in a Forest of Brevity

A threadbare thought, pulled and spun,
Dangles from branches, teasing for fun.
A rabbit hops by, with a cheeky grin,
In a world of whispers, he dances in.

The grass giggles, tickled by breeze,
While ants conspire with crafty ease.
Barely a word, just a smirk so sly,
In witty exchanges, they flutter and fly.

Mossy pillows host a slumbering snail,
Dreaming of journeys on a wandering trail.
With a flip of a leaf, a punchline disguised,
In this forest joke, wisdom's surprised.

For laughter grows wild, in every nook,
In the threads of thought that nature took.
So join in the fun, don't hold your breath,
In brevity's gift, we dance, not fret.

The Language of Bark and Brief

Bark speaks softly with knotted lore,
Telling tales where creatures explore.
With each tiny bump, a giggle stirs,
In the intricate knots, more laughter blurs.

A rabbit snickers, his ears a-twitch,
At the clumsy mole that lost his niche.
In whispers of night, the owls hoot clear,
Each bark a joke for those who hear.

Branches lean in with secrets to share,
As vines tangle up in a comical snare.
Nature's own script, a punchy affair,
Laughter and joy dance on warm summer air.

So listen closely to the forest's mirth,
In the language of bark, we find our worth.
With brevity mastered, and humor alive,
In glades where we gather, giggles thrive.

Brief Memories of the Whispering Wind

A zephyr hums a silly tune,
As leaves sway like a dancing loon.
It tickles ears, a playful tease,
Whisking past with mischievous ease.

A gust of laughter fills the glade,
Old branches creak, their jokes displayed.
They gossip low, with breezy cheer,
Spreading stories for all to hear.

The wind then trips on a twiggy friend,
Who rolls his eyes, as if to send,
A wink and nod, an inside joke,
As nature giggles, with no custom cloak.

In whispered rhymes, the air does sing,
About the pranks of every spring.
While nature laughs, we join in too,
As memories dance on winds so blue.

Shadows and Shards of Narratives

In twilight's grip, the tales unfold,
With shadows shifting, stories told.
Leaves whisper secrets, lost in time,
Each shard reflects a moment's rhyme.

Underneath the moon's soft gaze,
A laughter echoes through the maze.
Squirrels chatter, plotting pranks,
With shadows joining in the shanks.

A rogue raccoon lifts an owl's hat,
With silly antics, what of that?
The trees just sway, they know the jest,
As night rolls on, it's quite the fest.

Around the fire, the figures dance,
In fractured light, they spin and prance.
Each tale a chuckle, a wink, a nod,
In nature's humor, we find a prod.

The Fabled Economy of Pines

In the market of trees, there's quite a show,
Where needles barter and branches glow.
A pine once claimed his bark was gold,
While squirrels scoff, their cheeks all rolled.

The saplings giggle at their heights,
Each new growth leading to funny sights.
With every wind, some branches sway,
Imagining riches they joke away.

Leaves take bets on weather's mood,
With whispers of rain, they get quite rude.
"We're richer than oaks!" they flail and boast,
While chipmunks laugh, enjoying the toast.

The pine cone stock drops, oh what a plight!
Nature's trading floor brings sheer delight.
With every season, the market spins,
In this fabled realm, everybody wins.

Fleeting Footnotes of Flora

In the garden's nook, whispers abound,
With petals giggling on soft ground.
Each blossom shares a comical quote,
As bees take notes, and crickets gloat.

"Roses are red, but violets are bold!"
The daisies chuckle, stories retold.
A tulip fumbles, brought low by dew,
While daisies poke fun; oh, what a view!

With every breeze, they banter and clash,
Fleeting footnotes in a colorful smash.
As nature's kids play hide and seek,
Their leafy laughter, a joyful peek.

As night draws close, they settle down,
With whispered tales, no hint of frown.
For laughter sings beneath the stars,
In flora's heart, we find the spar.

Rustic Rhymes of the Evergreens

In the woods where pine trees sway,
A squirrel thinks it's time to play,
He dances round on branches high,
    Chasing shadows in the sky.

A wooden stump with tales to tell,
Of woodpeckers who ring the bell,
    The owls gossip in the night,
While raccoons plan their heist in fright.

The wind whispers jokes through the leaves,
As nature tricks, and mischief weaves,
A laugh erupts from a hidden nook,
    As critters gather for a look.

With twinkling stars in skies so vast,
The forest echoes tales from the past,
And if you pause and lend an ear,
You'll hear the giggles, loud and clear.

The Language of Leafy Silence

Beneath the branches, a rabbit sits,
With a carrot crown, he thinks he's it,
He hops along in foolish pride,
While hiding hard from what might slide.

A butterfly wearing shoes too bright,
Flaps and flutters, a comical sight,
He trips on petals, lands on his face,
And blinks in shock at his clumsy grace.

In the shade, a tortoise rolls,
While cherry ants steal jelly rolls,
All is silent but the chuckles near,
As nature's humor draws us near.

The wind giggles, a friendly tease,
Telling stories through rustling leaves,
In this green world of silly cheer,
Life dances with laughter, far and near.

Breezes and Brevities

A breeze comes by with a ticklish tone,
Playing tag with a dandelion blown,
The seeds scatter, a fluffy flight,
As they dance and giggle through the night.

The ants hold meetings in a wee cranny,
Debating lunch—how about a fanny?
They sip on dew, jesting about,
While under the moon, they twist and shout.

A deer walks in, styling a grin,
With leafy threads, oh where to begin?
His friends all gather, but hold their breath,
As the wise old owl croaks a jest of death.

The sun beams down, pulling shadows wide,
While squirrels compete on branches side by side,
Nature's comedy unfolds so sly,
In the embrace of the open sky.

Fleeting Thoughts Beneath the Canopy

Under branches, a wise one naps,
Dreams of snacks and funny mishaps,
The fox tiptoes, like a clumsy fool,
Stumbling over his very own rule.

Mice tell tales of their daring tricks,
How they sneak cheese, and play little flicks,
With laughter echoing, they sneak and hide,
While shadows chase them, side by side.

A crow caws loudly, sharing his jest,
Mocking a cat who failed her quest,
The leaves ignite in a rustling cheer,
As a giggling breeze brings all near.

In this jungle, with humor grand,
Even trees scratch their bark and stand,
For nature's spirit, so light and fleet,
Makes the mundane feel quite neat.

Fragments of Frayed Dreams

In a garden of wishes, where shadows play,
The gnomes throw a party at the break of day.
They dance on the grass with a wobble and spin,
While squirrels critique them wearing cheeky grins.

The sun peeks in, with a giggle and tease,
As daisies debate the best kind of cheese.
The wind winks and whispers, 'This fun can't last!'
But the laughter is swift, and the moments are vast.

A butterfly flutters, a jester on wing,
Forgetting it's supposed to be something of spring.
It lands with a thump, a curious sight,
While tulips erupt in laughter and light.

The clock rolls its eyes, but can't make a sound,
As free-spirited flowers all dance round and round.
And dreams take a break from being so grand,
To frolic in folly, unplanned and unplanned.

Echoes in the Underbrush

In the thicket, where whispers and chuckles reside,
A hedgehog tells tales of his journey with pride.
He pokes fun at the fox, in a splendid tuxedo,
As raccoons roll laughter like a well-worn burrito.

The owls hoot softly, their wisdom at bay,
When the crickets join in with the evening ballet.
They joke about night, and who's first to regret,
For snoozing too long, oh, what a regret!

A sneaky old snail slides in with a grin,
Declaring that patience is always a win.
But the shadows just snicker, and then drift away,
Leaving echoes on leaves, where the merriment lay.

With a rustle and shuffle, the night takes its call,
As laughter persists through the curtain of thrall.
The underbrush chuckles, concealed and free,
Where secrets and smiles blend in perfect glee.

Petals and Phrases Intertwined

In a field where oddities dangerously bloom,
Petals recite poetry, much to the gloom.
The daisies declare they're poets profound,
While marigolds giggle, their laughter unbound.

A bee with a monocle buzzes for style,
Claiming rhymes are his game, at least for a while.
He drifts through each stanza, as flowery wit,
Composes a ballet of verses that split.

With whispers of breezes, the flowers converse,
About cosmic events and the latest in verse.
The poppies all debate the best type of soap,
While the violets ponder, 'Is dreaming a trope?'

In this fragrant soiree, the humor is ripe,
As sunbeams cast laughter in golden type.
Each phrase a bouquet, all wondrously twined,
In the garden of giggles, where good times unwind.

Whispered Secrets of the Woodland

Amidst ancient trees with their branches entwined,
The woodland reveals what it cleverly lined.
A rabbit with glasses recites with a flair,
While mushrooms are nodding, all caught in the air.

The owls hoot gossip, in whispers so sly,
About acorns that fell and who thought to fly.
Each leaf carries tales of sheer ridiculous fates,
As beetles reenact their adventurous states.

With shadows like giggles that dance on the ground,
The breeze carries chuckles, a soft, silly sound.
The pinecones are perched, like a wise council crew,
Spinning stories of wonder, with humor in view.

For nature's a jokester, in dapple and shade,
In a world where the laughter is never delayed.
The woodland confesses, with glee, not despair,
That secrets are sweeter when shared everywhere.

Shards of Silence and Substance

In a world of quiet tweets,
The squirrels hold board meetings.
Imaginary nut fees,
While the wind just keeps giggling.

A raindrop's splash brings a grin,
Little worms dance on the skin.
Nature's joke, sly and sweet,
Beware of mud beneath the feet!

Sticks debate, poke, and prod,
Tree roots joke about the sod.
Their laughter travels through the air,
Making you stop and stare.

So next time you're out and about,
Listen close, there's fun no doubt.
Nature's antics at every bend,
From bushes green, you'll have a friend.

Subtle Scribbles in the Underbrush

A beetle writes a tiny blog,
On the back of a gray frog.
They share tales of daily runs,
And the tricks they play on the sun.

Grass blades pirouette with flair,
In breezy typo-dancing air.
Each twist and turn, a new delight,
Frogs giggle at the night's first light.

Bunnies gossip 'neath the moon,
Whiskers twitching to a tune.
The bushes chuckle, lush and loud,
With secrets shared, they feel so proud.

So if you wander off the path,
You might just catch a glimpse of wrath.
In the scribbles of the night,
There's humor in the dimming light.

Short Strokes on Gnarled Roots

Roots are artists, painting jibes,
Each twist a joke that thrives.
They sketch with soil, their favorite ink,
Telling stories that make you think.

A porcupine's quill sparks a laugh,
While owls on branches draft their graph.
Lines of wit twine 'round the tree,
Drawing chuckles from you and me.

Nature's palette is bold and bright,
With grins hidden from our sight.
Gnarled tales of playful trees,
Invite you in to join with ease.

So seek the roots that pave your way,
In their humor, you'll want to stay.
Each gnarled turn whispers a pun,
Reminding us that life is fun!

Leafy Brevity and Poetic Twists

Leaves whisper secrets while dancing,
Twirling like they're romancing.
With every flap, a giggly jest,
Trees laugh hard, they know the best.

A pebble winks at a passing breeze,
While ants march on, doing as they please.
Mischief is ripe on this grassy floor,
Tickled by sunshine, they ask for more.

Frogs leap in a rhythm absurd,
Croaking puns that leave them stirred.
A river chuckles, flowing on by,
Telling tales with a glint in its eye.

So pause for a moment, enjoy the game,
In nature's heart, nothing's the same.
Each twist and turn is a laugh to share,
Inviting us all to join in the flair.

Poetic Twists

In the glen where the shadows dance,
Mice don bowties, give life a chance.
A cat with a monocle, wise and sly,
Plans an extravaganza, oh my, oh my!

The daisies gossip, sharing tales,
Of travelers caught in spunky gales.
While crickets sing with laughter's bite,
Calling for joy under the moonlit night.

Each twig and leaf is in on the game,
Crafting capers that kindle the flame.
In the humor of earth, there's no disguise,
Playful spirit that always flies.

So step in the blur of glee's embrace,
Nature's giggles will quicken your pace.
With joy in your heart, take a chance to twirl,
Join the frolic—the world's a whirl!

Musings in Minimalism

A single leaf jumps high,
A shadow under the sky.
It whispers secrets to the breeze,
While squirrels giggle in the trees.

A paper clip's a lovely crown,
For all the ants that march in town.
They salute with tiny wee salute,
As if they wear a fancy suit.

In this world of little things,
A biscuit's what a crow now swings.
Crumbs fall down like whispers loud,
A feast beneath the laughing cloud.

The sun peeks through a branch or two,
Painting shadows all askew.
Life's odd in a simple frame,
Yet somehow it's a funny game.

The Rustic Register of Wander

A pebble rolls beneath my shoe,
It chuckles at the sky so blue.
The grass sings softly, proud and bright,
An acorn plans a daring flight.

The map is lost, but who needs those?
With every step, a tiny pose.
A snail's parade is on full spree,
I'm late for tea, but oh, dear me!

A wanderer's hat flies off with glee,
Chasing a wind as wild as me.
The path is a jolly jigsaw, see,
Every turn a new surprise, whee!

With trails that twist like noodle dreams,
And ponds that dance in silver gleams.
Nature grins; it knows the trick,
Life's a joke that's mighty slick.

The Essence of the Ethereal Green

Oh, the grass hums a silly tune,
Beneath a laughing, golden moon.
A worm wears shades; it's quite the sight,
As daisies wink with pure delight.

The clouds are marshmallows in disguise,
They float along with goofy sighs.
Each raindrop bounces, full of cheer,
While frogs practice their karaoke here.

A butterfly flutters with flair and grace,
Challenging the snail to a silly race.
Their rivalry, oh, what a jest,
Both think they are the very best.

In the glade, laughter fills the air,
Nature's jokes are everywhere.
With every giggle, dreams can gleam,
We dance along the whimsical stream.

Nature's Quiet Chronicles

The tree lines whisper tales of cheer,
A breeze giggles, drawing near.
A spider's web in morning light,
Is a masterpiece of pure delight.

The brook chuckles with a splash,
While pebbles dance, oh what a bash!
A duck parade in a single line,
Feathers fluffed, feeling divine.

A rock sits still, but has a tale,
Of rainy days and storms that hail.
Mossy secrets wrapped so tight,
Every green patch a pure delight.

Nature laughs, it's quite the muse,
Playing tricks like it can choose.
With every chirp and rustle near,
Life's a pun, let out a cheer!

The Neatly Pruned Prose of the Grove

In a well-kept garden, the jokes grow tall,
They giggle and wiggle, they never fall.
Each line a stem, trimmed just right,
Creating a smile, like sunshine bright.

With patches of puns in every row,
The humor in nature begins to flow.
Blossoms that chuckle, leaves that snicker,
Sprouting up laughter, just a bit quicker.

Watch out for weeds that might pull a prank,
They'll sneak up on you, but give them a spank!
For nature thrives where chuckles dwell,
In the grove of giggles, all is well.

When the sun sets low, and shadows play,
The trees share secrets in a funny way.
They rustle their leaves, a leafy choir,
Musing on humor, never to tire.

Fragments of Lyrical Leaves

Leaves flutter by, with tales to tell,
Whispering secrets, casting a spell.
In the breeze, they dance and tease,
Crafting a story with every sneeze.

Petals drop down like punchlines sweet,
Falling in rhythm to the skip of feet.
A giggle caught in the rustling air,
Lyrical moments, floating without a care.

Puddles of laughter, like dew they shine,
Each droplet's a jest, oh so divine!
Wobbling branches like a stand-up show,
Cracking up all in the sunlight's glow.

Here's to the whims of the breezy day,
Where laughter runs wild, come what may.
Fragmented lives come together bright,
In the realms of nature, pure delight.

The Unadorned Ballads of the Brambles

In the thickets deep, where brambles thrive,
Songs of the wild keep humor alive.
Each berry a note, plucked with a grin,
Singing the tales of where they've been.

The branches entwined, like laughter spun,
A balled-up jest, and oh what fun!
They tickle your ears with riddles in lace,
While thorns draw a smile across every face.

With whispers of sass that the wind brings near,
They joke about thorns and splinters, my dear.
In the heart of the brambles, where mischief sleeps,
Lies a funny saga the forest keeps.

So here's to the trails of the wild and free,
Where brambles weave tales, humorously!
Each barbed branch offers a chuckle or two,
In the unadorned ballads, pure and true.

Raindrops and Riddles

Raindrops fall down like riddles from skies,
Puddles reflect all the silly replies.
With splashes of laughter, the play begins,
As nature spins tales on weathered spins.

Umbrellas bloom like flowers in dance,
Each one an inch of its droll little prance.
While rivers chuckle and mud banks grumble,
The comedy rains and we all just tumble.

When lightning strikes like a punchline bold,
The thunder speaks jokes, a tale retold.
In the theater of storms, laughs intertwine,
A splash of delight, this chaos divine.

So when rain starts to fall, don't frown or pout,
Just wet your whistle and join in the rout!
For riddles of raindrops are bound to amuse,
In the joyful downpour, we'll never lose!

Sparse Verses and Nature's Secrets

In the garden, weeds wear crowns,
Bouncing beans in silly gowns.
Trees chuckle with a rustling sound,
While flowers play hide and seek around.

Bees buzz jokes in syrupy lines,
Dandelions dance, sipping on wines.
Nature's secret, a chuckling breeze,
Mischief twinkles in the swaying trees.

Squirrels gossip, nibble on seeds,
Chasing shadows with silly deeds.
Rabbits hop, clutching their hats,
While the sun dips down, whispering chats.

Nature's humor in every nook,
Listen close, come take a look.
Laughter lingers in chirpy notes,
As clouds create the silliest floats.

Rustic Echoes in Trimmed Phrasing

At dawn, the rooster sings off-key,
While goats dance with absolute glee.
Leaves clap hands like a cheering crowd,
As the old oak tree stands so proud.

The creek giggles, skipping through stones,
Frogs add rhythm with ribbeting tones.
A snail slips out, wearing a tie,
Each leaf whispers, 'Oh my, oh my!'

Chickens gossip, pecking for jokes,
While turtles snicker, avoiding folks.
Cows moo musings, wise and absurd,
In this pastoral world, laughter's inferred.

Rustic life, with its quirky charms,
Nature's humor spreads its arms.
Each creature plays a role in jest,
In this earthy stage, we're all guests.

Beneath the Canopy of Conciseness

Under branches, shadows dance,
A squirrel waves, a cheeky glance.
Mice tell tales with tiny specks,
While ants parade in mismatched specs.

Clouds roll in with playful sighs,
Tickling the grasses, oh how they rise!
Sunbeams giggle, slipping through leaves,
As the world hums, and mischief weaves.

A fox in socks steals a glance,
While crickets chirp in a wild prance.
Each rustle beckons a playful tune,
Underneath the fast-whispering moon.

Nature hides jokes, just out of sight,
In every bush, a playful light.
So join the fun, don't be a bore,
There's laughter waiting behind each door.

Nature's Haikus on a Whispering Wind

Fluffy clouds in rows,
Frogs leap, causing giggles,
Nature's secrets flow.

Dewdrops like laughter,
Sunshine tickles sleepy blooms,
Joy in every breath.

Breezes share the news,
Butterflies whisper along,
Dancing through the trees.

Twigs weave silly tales,
Wandering paths where frogs dine,
Nature's prose compiled.

www.ingramcontent.com/pod-product-compliance
Lightning Source LLC
Chambersburg PA
CBHW071814160426
43209CB00003B/88